Trivia for Smart Kids!

Over 300 Questions About Animals, Bugs, Nature, Space, Math, Movies and So Much More (Part 1)

DL Digital Entertainment

TABLE OF CONTENTS

SPECIAL BONUS!

Want These 2 Bonus Books for FREE?

 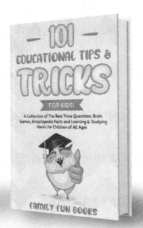

Get FREE, unlimited access to these and all of our new books by joining our community!

SCAN w/ your camera TO JOIN!

INTRODUCTION

We would like to personally thank you for taking the time to purchase our book *Trivia for Smart Kids Pt. 1.* We have spent countless hours putting together only the best and most interesting trivia questions for you, the kids and the entire family to enjoy! You can expect to find 250+ different trivia questions ranging from categories such as: Math, History, Geography, Animals, Bugs, T.V. Shows, Movies, Nature, Science and Sports. These trivia questions are guaranteed to make you and your kids think hard and have all kinds of fun while doing so.

Trivia for Smart Kids Pt. 1 is very versatile thanks to being in audio format as well on Audible.com! Use it on your own before bed, with friends at a get together, with family at the dinner table or camping with relatives; the possibilities with it are endless. Be creative and utilize it to its full potential!

WHY TRIVIA QUESTIONS?

This amazing assortment of trivia questions will not only test your children, but you and your family members in a fun and interactive way. The art of Trivia has been around for a lot longer than you might think and has many other benefits such as:

-Confidence Boosting: *With so many kids and people in general struggling with self-confidence in our day and age, doing these trivia questions in a safe environment with family and friends can give them the opportunity to comfortably answer, even though they might be wrong, helping them to not be afraid to express themselves.*

-Improved Bonding: *Trivia For Smart Kids is one of the best ways for friends and family to spend time with each other and build positive, healthy relationships through teamwork and encouragement when trying to solve the trivia questions found in this book.*

*-**Reading Comprehension Skills:** Trivia Questions are oftentimes written in slightly more challenging words and phrases in order to test the listener and make them think. Having children listen to them throughout this book significantly helps improve their reading skills and comprehension.*

*-**Reduce Boredom:** Having an audiobook such as Trivia For Smart Kids gives you the ability to have fun and entertainment on demand. Since we provide it in audiobook form, you can utilize it in any situation you can think of!*

*-**Improve Concentration:** Children - and many adults – often suffer from a lack of focus and struggle to concentrate for long periods of time. These Trivia questions will force you to focus 100% in order to come up with solutions to them, sufficiently boosting overall personal concentration and focus levels.*

Now, that's enough talking. Are you ready to get started with *Trivia For Smart Kids?*

Awesome! Let's Begin.

ANIMAL TRIVIA

"If having a soul means being able to feel love, loyalty and gratitude, then animals are better off than a lot of humans" - James Herriot

1. Which of the following dogs is the smallest?

    A) Dachshund

    B) Poodle

    C) Pomeranian

    D) Chihuahua

Answer: D, the smallest dog breed is the chihuahua

2. What color are zebras?

A) White with black stripes.

B) Black with white stripes.

C) Both of the above.

D) None of the above.

Answer: B, zebras have a black base with white stripes.

3. What is the biggest animal on our planet?

A) Blue whale

B) African elephant

C) Giraffe

D) Gray Whale

Answer: A, the Blue Whale is the largest animal currently on the planet

4. Which of the following animals sleep standing up?

A) Gorillas

B) Flamingos

C) Camels

D) Ravens

Answer: B, flamingos sleep standing up because the salt flats they live on are too caustic to sit down in.

5. What is the fastest water animal?

A) Porpoise

B) Sailfish

C) Flying fish

D) Tuna

Answer: B, the sailfish is the fastest water animal, reaching speeds up to 68 miles per hour.

6. Which of the following animal groups does a zebra belong to?

A) Horse

B) Dog

C) Cat

D) Rat

Answer: A, zebras belong to the horse family.

7. How many teeth are baby horses born with?

A) 2

B) 10

C) 6

D) 0

Answer: D, baby horses' teeth don't show up until about a week after birth

8. Gorillas live in groups called:

A) Squads

B) Gangs

C) Troops

D) Crews

Answer: B, they live in groups called Troops

9. What are baby meerkats called?

A) Katlets

B) Moogs

C) Meeks

D) Pups

Answer: D, baby meerkats are called pups

10. When a baby great white shark is born, how long does it stay with its mother?

A) 1 month

B) 6 months

C) 0 days

D) 1 year

Answer: C, it leaves its mother immediately

11. What is the typical lifespan of a great white shark?

A) 10 years

B) 20 years

C) 30 years

D) 40 years

Answer: C, 30 years

12. On average, how long do lions spend eating each day?

A) 15 minutes

B) 1 hour

C) 2 hours

D) 5 hours

Answer: B, they spend about 1 hour each day eating

13. What is the correct name for an adult female horse?

A) Filly

B) Mare

C) Colt

D) Lon

Answer: B, they are called Mares

14. Elephants walk quite slowly, approximately 4 mph, but how fast can they run if they are excited or scared?

A.   20 mph
B.   30 mph
C.   40 mph
D.   50 mph

Answer: B, 30 mph is the speed elephants can run at

15. Us humans have just two sets of teeth in our lifetime

but a shark continuously produces new teeth and 'sheds' old teeth throughout its life. How many teeth might a shark grow, use and then shed each year?

A.   60 teeth
B.   600 teeth
C.   6000 teeth
D.   10 teeth

Answer: C, 6000 teeth, this is why fossilized shark teeth are extremely common.

16. How many different species of fish are there?

A.   310
B.   2100
C.   27000
D.   100000

Answer: C, there are 27000 different species of fish to date!

17. How much water can a fully grown rhinoceros drink per day?

A.   100 litres
B.   1000 litres
C.   500 litres
D.   50 litres

Answer: A, a fully grown rhino can drink up to 100 litres of water per day.

18. On average, how much does a fully grown adult elephant weigh?

A.   1 ton
B.   2 tons
C.   5 tons
D.   0.5 tons

Answer: B, a fully grown elephant weighs approximately 2 tons

19. Which of these animals walks like a camel?

A.   Giraffe
B.   Dog
C.   Cat
D.   Elephant

Answer: A, giraffes and camels walk by moving both legs on one side and then both legs on the other side!

20. What bird's eyes are larger than its brain?

A.   Eagle
B.   Owl
C.   Ostrich
D.   Parrot

Answer: C, ostrich's eyes are larger than their brains

21. Which animal can look two ways at the same time?

A.   Chameleon
B.   Lizard
C.   Snake
D.   Tortoise

Answer: A, the chameleon has the ability to look two ways at one time

22. What is a mole's main source of food?

A.   Ladybugs
B.   Ants
C.   Snails
D.   Earthworms

Answer: D, earthworms are a mole's main source of food

23. What is the name for a group of frogs?

A.   Troop
B.   Squad
C.   Army
D.   Force

Answer: C, a group of frogs is called an army

24. What is a fox's den called?

A.   Home
B.   Shelter
C.   Cave
D.   Earth

Answer: D, a foxes den is really called an 'Earth'

25. Walt Disney's famous deer was named what?

A.   Lily
B.   Ariel
C.   Nala
D.   Bambi

Answer: D, the famous deer was named Bambi

26. Which animal has rectangular pupils?

A.   Horse
B.   Deer
C.   Goat
D.   Llama

Answer: C, a goat has rectangular pupils, how crazy is that?!

27. What is the largest land animal?

A.   Giraffe
B.   Elephant
C.   Moose
D.   Rhino

Answer: B, the largest land animal is the elephant

28. What animal pollinates banana plants in the wild?

A.   Bees
B.   Flies
C.   Bats
D.   Hummingbirds

Answer: C, surprisingly enough, bats pollinate banana plants in the wild!

29. Which one of these animals can freeze without dying?

A.   Frogs
B.   Birds
C.   Turtles
D.   Fish

Answer: A, a number of studies have shown that frogs can live through being frozen...

30. What is the name for the study of animals?

A.   Entomology
B.   Biology
C.   Mammalogy
D.   Zoology

Answer: D, zoology is the study of animals

31. What is the correct number of living species that have been identified?

A.   More than 10 million
B.   More than 100 million
C.   More than 1 million
D.   More than 50 million

Answer: C, more than 1 million living species of animals have been identified during our time spent on earth

32. The main definition of an "animal" is that it:

A.   Is mobile during at least one phase of its life
B.   Has fur, claws, paws, fins, or blubber
C.   Can manufacture its own energy through the processing of organic or inorganic material
D.   Has four limbs or more

Answer: A, it has to be able to move about under its own power (be mobile) during a stage of its life, unlike plants and fungi

BUG AND INSECT TRIVIA

1. How do bees communicate with one another?

A.   Talking
B.   Dancing
C.   Flying
D.   Buzzing

Answer: B, bees communicate by something called a Waggle Dance

2. On a common ladybug, what color are the spots?

A.   Orange
B.   Red
C.   White
D.   Black

Answer: D, the spots on a common ladybug are black

3. Of these four bugs, which one has teeth?

A.   Flies
B.   Mosquitos
C.   Beetles
D.   Bees

Answer: B, yes, mosquitos have tiny teeth used to cut through skin and even protective layers of clothing

4. How many people do stinging insects send to the emergency room every year?

A.   500
B.   30000
C.   200000
D.   More than 500000

Answer: D, 500,000 or more people get sent to the ER for anything from fire ants to wasps and yellow jackets which can all cause dangerous allergic reactions

5. Insects make up:

A.   Only a small group of the world's creatures
B.   Most of the world's creatures
C.   A group of creatures that only live in tropical regions
D.   A moderate percentage of the world's creatures

Answer: B, insects make up the majority of our world's creatures (roughly 70 - 80%!)

6. Insects have at least:

A.   Four legs
B.   Eight legs
C.   Six legs
D.   Two legs

Answer: C, to be considered an insect, they must have 6 legs or more!

7. What does the monarch butterfly do in the winter time?

A.   Flies to warm places
B.   Stays near oceans and coastal regions
C.   It always stays in tropical regions
D.   It flies north

Answer: A, the monarch butterfly seeks out warm places during the winter time

8. The legs of an insect are joined to its:

A.   Head
B.   Abdomen
C.   Both abdomen and thorax
D.   Thorax

Answer: D, insects' legs are always joined at the thorax

9. The three insect body parts include:

A.   Head, neck, abdomen
B.   Head, thorax, abdomen
C.   Head, abdomen, tail
D.   Head, body, tail

Answer: B, an insect's 3 main body parts are its head, thorax and abdomen

10. Which of the following is not considered an insect and

better considered a bug?

A.   Grasshopper
B.   Butterfly
C.   Beetle
D.   Centipede

Answer: D, centipedes have too many legs to be considered an insect

11. Which of the following insects has not evolved much from its original form?

A.   Cockroach
B.   Dragonfly
C.   Dung Beetle
D.   Ant

Answer: A, fossil records show that insects existed 390 million years ago. Some of the earliest insects, such as cockroaches, have changed very little

12. What body part do insects use to sense things?

A.   Thorax

B.   Antennae
C.   Wings
D.   Exoskeleton

Answer: B, insects use their antennae to sense the world around them!

13. Insects do indeed have eyes. What is the main purpose of them?

A.   Detecting colors
B.   Detecting light
C.   Detecting smell
D.   Magnifying images

Answer: B, the simple eyes, or ocelli, are located on the head between the compound eyes. The ocelli aren't used for vision, but to detect changes in the intensity of light

14. Which vital body part (in humans), do insects not have?

A.   Heart
B.   Feat
C.   Esophagus
D.   Lungs

Answer: D, on insects, a system of branching air tubes, or tracheae, reaches all parts of the body. Air enters through openings called spiracles

15. What percentage of insects are harmful to plants and animals?

A.   10 percent
B.   4 percent
C.   2 percent
D.   30 percent

Answer: C, less than 2 percent of all insect species are harmful; but among them, they can cause major crop damage and spread serious diseases

16. Which of the following is a sign that an insect is probably safe to eat?

A.   Hairy body
B.   Dull coloration
C.   Long antennae
D.   Has wings

Answer: B, a general rule of thumb is not to eat any

brightly colored insects since it's nature's way of warning predators that this insect is poisonous

17. The term "bug" describes a certain type of insect. What do bugs have that other insects don't have?

A.   Ridges on all six legs
B.   Compound eyes
C.   Piercing and sucking mouthparts
D.   Antennae

Answer: C, bugs have piercing and sucking mouthparts

18. What kind of insects make up 40% of all described insects?

A.   Bees
B.   Beetles
C.   Mosquitos
D.   Ladybugs

Answer: B, beetles make up 40% of all described insects!

19. Crickets are famous for chirping, but how do they make that noise?

A.   Rubbing their legs together
B.   Whistling through their mandibles
C.   Jumping into the air
D.   Rubbing against each other

Answer: A, crickets make their signature noise by rubbing their legs together.

20. What is the biggest insect ever discovered?

A.   The Giant Weta
B.   The Hercules Beetle
C.   The Madagascar Walking Stock
D.   The Dung Beetle

Answer: A, the Giant Weta is the biggest insect ever discovered. It looks like a mixture between a giant cricket and a spider!

21. What insect is the fastest runner?

A.   Dung Beetle
B.   Fire Ant
C.   Harvester Ant
D.   Cockroach

Answer: D, the cockroach is the fastest running insect

22. What is the name for the middle segment of an insect's body?

A.   Abdomen
B.   Phalange
C.   Thorax
D.   Antennae

Answer: C, the thorax is the middle region of an insect's body

23. Insects live all over the world. What is the only continent where insects do not live?

A.   Australia
B.   Antarctica
C.   Asia
D.   Canada

Answer: B, it is much too cold for insects to live and thrive in Antarctica

24. Butterflies taste with their:

A.   Wings
B.   Feet
C.   Antennae
D.   Eyes

Answer: B, surprisingly enough, butterflies taste things with their feet!

25. Dung beetles roll their turd balls:

A.   In a straight line
B.   1 foot left, then 1 foot right
C.   1 foot left then back 1 foot, then straight
D.   2 feet left and 2 feet right

Answer: A, Dung beetles roll them primarily straight and never according to exact measurement

26. How many stomachs to ants have?

A.   4
B.   6
C.   1

D.   2

Answer: D, ants have 2 stomachs; one to hold the food for themselves and the other stomach for fellow ants!

27. Crickets are considered _____ in some parts of the world

A.   Good luck
B.   Bad luck
C.   Money
D.   Evil

Answer: A, in the Far East and well across Europe, it is considered very bad luck to kill a cricket, even by accident, and it's considered good luck to see one

28. Which mosquitoes are the ones that feed on blood?

A.   Male
B.   Female
C.   Brown
D.   Red

Answer: B, female mosquitoes are the only ones in the family to feed on blood

29. What is a baby grasshopper called?

A.   Hopper
B.   Youngin
C.   Larva
D.   Nymph

Answer: D, baby grasshoppers are called Nymphs

30. 'Bee Killer' refers to what kind of insect?

A.   Spider
B.   Wasp
C.   Fly
D.   Ant

Answer: C, flies are referred to as 'Bee Killers'

31. Where are crickets' ears located?

A.   Head
B.   Feet
C.   Front legs

D.   Rear abdomen

Answer: C, crickets' ears are surprisingly found on the front legs! How interesting...

T.V. AND MOVIE TRIVIA

"Movies touch our hearts, and awaken our vision, and change the way we see things. They take us to other places. They open doors and minds. Movies are the memories of our lifetime, we need to keep them alive." - Martin Scorsese

1. In the movie 'Toy Story' to whom does Woody belong?

A.   Andy
B.   Sid
C.   Buzz
D.   Billy

Answer: A, Woody belonged to Andy in the Toy story movies

2. In the movie 'Peter Pan' who is Captain Hook's pirate-buddy?

A.   Smee
B.   Big Chef
C.   Peter
D.   Tink

Answer: A, Smee is the little chubby pirate who Hook bosses around

3. In the movie 'Aladdin' who does Jasmine meet in the marketplace?

A.   Her father
B.   The genie
C.   Her mother
D.   Aladdin

Answr: D, Jasmine and Aladdin meet for the first time when she sneaks out to the marketplace

4. In the movie 'The Little Mermaid' what is Ariel's little fish friend's name?

A.   Chip
B.   Flounder
C.   Sebastian
D.   Eric

Answer: B, Flounder is Ariel's little yellow fish buddy

5. Which of these is NOT one of the seven dwarves in Snow White?

A.   Sleepy
B.   Dopey
C.   Bashful
D.   Smiley

Answer: D, the seven dwarves were: Doc, Sneezy, Dopey, Bashful, Grumpy, Sleepy, and Happy

6. In the TV show 'Catdog' what are Dog's favorite foods?

A.   Tacos with hot sauce
B.   Hot dogs with ketchup
C.   Fish with tartar sauce
D.   Vegetables with cheese sauce

Answer: A, Dog eats the super hot tacos and sauce and then Cat has to suffer!

7. Who lives in a pineapple under the sea?

A.   Catdog
B.   The wild Thornberrys
C.   Doug
D.   Spongebob SquarePants

Answer: D, Spongebob SquarePants lives in a pineapple under the sea!

8. On the show 'Sabrina the Teenage Witch' what is the name of Sabrina's cat?

A.   Salem
B.   Blackie
C.   Warlock
D.   Helga

Answer: A, Salem is a warlock who was turned into a cat and can't change back

9. In the movie 'Annie', what is Annie's dog's name?

A.   Sandy
B.   Rover
C.   Champion
D.   Lady

Answer: A, Annie names him Sandy because he's the color of sand

10. On the cartoon 'Recess' who is the ruler of the playground?

A.   Prince Will
B.   King Bob
C.   King Dave
D.   Gus

Answer: B, King Bob was the supreme ruler of the playground!

11. In the movie 'ET' what does Elliot dress up ET as for Halloween to get him out of the house without his Mom seeing?

A.   A ghost with clown feet
B.   A monster with boots
C.   A hunchback with sneakers
D.   A skeleton with no feet

Answer: A, they put a sheet over ET and clown shoes on his feet. Elliot's Mom thinks ET is Gertie, but he's not!

12. What is the name of the show that has these characters on it? Slippery Soap, Paprika, and Magenta.

A.   Gullah Gullah Island
B.   Barney
C.   Eureka's Castle
D.   Blue's Clues

Answer: D, Blue's Clues has these characters on it!

13. Who is Franklin's Friend who is hungry almost all the time?

A.   Snail
B.   Beaver
C.   Bear
D.   Fox

Answer: C, Bear is always hungry in the show Franklin!

14. What were the little people called in "Willy Wonka and the Chocolate Factory"?

A.   Dwarfs
B.   Oompa-Loompas
C.   Munchkins
D.   Fidgets

Answer: B, the little people in the movie were called Oompa-Loompas

15. In which 2001 movie did Eddie Murphy play the character Donkey?

A.   Shrek
B.   The Lion King
C.   Lilo & Stitch
D.   Tarzan

Answer: A, he played Donkey in Shrek

16. What movie sequel about a mouse was released in 2002?

A.   Lilo & Stitch
B.   Ice Age
C.   Stuart Little 2
D.   Scooby-Doo

Answer: C, Stuart Little starred a mouse and his child companion George

17. What's the title of the original animated movie about a time when the Earth was overrun by glaciers?

A.   The Emperor's New Groove
B.   Ice Age
C.   The Powerpuff Girls Movie
D.   Toy Story

Answer: B, Ice Age was based around the time that Earth was overrun by glaciers

18. In which 2001 movie did John Goodman voice the character the big blue not-so-mean monster, Sulley?

A.   Monsters, Inc.
B.   An American Tale
C.   Happy Feet
D.   Toy Story

Answer: A, Monsters, Inc. was the movie that featured John Goodman's Character Sulley

19. In "Land Before Time II" and "V" what character did Littlefoot and his friends see a lot?

A.   The Two Threehorn Twins
B.   Chomper
C.   Monster
D.   Lee

Answer: B, Littlefoot and his friends always seemed to see Chomper

20. Where was it that the Grinch stole Christmas from?

A.   Whoville
B.   Whereville
C.   Whatville
D.   Whosland

Answer: A, Whoville is where the Grinch stole Christmas from

21. What film features the animated characters Lola and Lenny?

A.   Shrek

B.   Ice Age
C.   Finding Nemo
D.   Shark Tale

Answer: D, the animated movie Shark Tale Features Lola and Lenny

22. Which film is about the son of a gangster shark boss?

A.   Are we there yet?
B.   Bee Movie
C.   Shark Tale
D.   Cars

Answer: C, Shark tale is about this!

23. What magical creatures lead Merida to a witch in 'Brave'?

A.   Goblins
B.   Will O' The Wisps
C.   Ghosts
D.   Selkies

Answer: B, Will O' The Wisps were the magical creatures that lead Merida to a witch

24. Who voiced Remy in 'Ratatouille'?

A.   David Cross
B.   Will Ferrell
C.   Adam Sandler
D.   Patton Oswalt

Answer: D, Patton Oswalt voiced Remy

25. What's the name of the ball with a star that appears in many Pixar films?

A.   Bouncers
B.   Andy's Ball
C.   The Luxo Ball
D.   The BNL Ball

Answer: C, the ball is called the Luxo ball!

26. What fraternity does Mike Wazowski join in 'Monsters University'?

A.   Roar Omega Roar
B.   Oozma Kappa

C.   Alpha Scarems
D.   Sigma Fear Omega

Answer: B, The fraternity Mike joins is called Oozma Kappa

27. In 'The Incredibles', before he became Syndrome, he wore rocket boots and called himself what?

A.   Incrediboy
B.   Incredikid
C.   Rocket Boy
D.   The Incredible Boy

Answer: A, Syndrome became known as Incrediboy

28. Who famously said, "To Infinity and Beyond" in 'Toy Story'?

A.   Andy
B.   Mr. Potato Head
C.   Rex
D.   Buzz Lightyear

Answer: D, Buzz Lightyear was a spaceman toy in Toy Story and famously said, "To Infinity and Beyond"

29. Who voiced Lightning McQueen in 'Cars'?

A.   Andy Samberg
B.   Ben Stiller
C.   Matt Damon
D.   Owen Wilson

Answer: D, Owen Wilson Voices Lighting McQueen. "Cah chow!"

30. On what planet was Wall-E stranded at the beginning of the movie 'Wall-E'?

A.   Saturn
B.   Mars
C.   Earth
D.   Venus

Answer: C, Wall-E was stranded on planet earth

31. In "Finding Nemo", who states that they have short term memory loss but still remembers some things?

A.   Crush
B.   Nemo
C.   Gill
D.   Dory

Answer: D, Dory is the one in "Finding Nemo" who has the bad memory

GEOGRAPHY TRIVIA

"Without geography, you're nowhere" - Unknown Author

1. Which country is Paris the capital of?

A.   Spain
B.   Canada
C.   France
D.   India

Answer: C, Paris is located in the country of France in Europe

2. What is the national capital city of Canada?

A.   Washington D.C.
B.   Ottawa
C.   Vancouver
D.   Seattle

Answer: B, Ottawa, located in the province of Ontario

3. What's the earth's largest continent?

A.   Antarctica
B.   Asia
C.   Europe
D.   North America

Answer: B, Asia is Earth's largest continent at approximately 17,300,000 square miles (44,806,812 sq km)

4. What razor-thin country accounts for more than half of the western coastline of South America?

A.   Ecuador
B.   Peru
C.   Bolivia
D.   Chile

Answer: D, Chile has a thin coastline of 2650 miles (4265 km) which accounts for more than half of the western coastline of South America

5. What country has the most natural lakes?

A.   Australia
B.   India
C.   Germany
D.   Canada

Answer: D, Canada has more than half of all the natural lakes in the world

6. What is the driest place on Earth?

A.   Sahara Desert
B.   Osoyoos, British Columbia
C.   McMurdo, Antarctica
D.   Death Valley, California

Answer: C, The driest place on Earth: the McMurdo Dry Valleys in Antarctica. Fun fact: It hasn't rained there for more than 2 million years!

7. Which African nation has the most pyramids?

A.   Egypt
B.   Sudan

C.   Algeria
D.   Libya

Answer: B, Sudan is home to over 200 pyramids

8. What African country served as the setting for Tatooine in Star Wars?

A.   Ethiopia
B.   Cape Town
C.   Gabon
D.   Tunisia

Answer: D, Tatooine was filmed in Tunisia, Africa

9. What is the oldest active volcano on Earth?

A.   Mt. Fuji
B.   Mt. Baker
C.   Mt. Yasur
D.   Mt. Etna

Answer: D, Mount Etna in Italy is thought to be the world's oldest active volcano

10. What city is the capital of Australia?

A.   Sydney
B.   Canberra
C.   Perth
D.   Melbourne

Answer: B, Canberra replaced Melbourne as the capital of Australia in 1908

11. What is the deepest point in Earth's oceans?

A.   Mariana Trench
B.   Tonga Trench
C.   Eurasian Basin
D.   Java Trench

Answer: A, the deepest part of the ocean is the Mariana Trench

12. What is the smallest state in the USA?

A.   Texas
B.   Idaho
C.   Washington

D.   Rhode Island

Answer: D, Rhode Island is the smallest state in the USA

13. What is the largest state in the USA by area?

A.   Alaska
B.   Texas
C.   California
D.   Arizona

Answer: A, Alaska is the biggest state by area in the USA

14. Where is the famous rock mural Mt. Rushmore located in the USA?

A.   North Dakota
B.   South Dakota
C.   Arizona
D.   Washington

Answer: B, Mt. Rushmore is located in South Dakota

15. What is the capital of Florida?

A.   Tampa Bay
B.   Miami
C.   Orlando
D.   Tallahassee

Answer: D, Tallahassee is the capital city of Florida, U.S.A.

16. What Australian city boasts the world's largest natural harbor?

A.   Melbourne
B.   Brisbane
C.   Perth
D.   Sydney

Answer: D, Sydney surrounds the world's largest natural harbor

17. What is the largest country in the world in terms of land area?

A.   United States
B.   Russia
C.   India
D.   Mexico

Answer: B, Russia is the largest country in the world, covering more than one eighth of Earth's inhabited land area

18. What is the longest mountain range in the world?

A.   The Andes
B.   The Rocky Mountains
C.   The Transantarctic Mountains
D.   The Himalayas

Answer: A, the Andes of South America is the longest mountain range in the world, stretching for an estimated distance of 7,000 km (4,350 miles)

19. What is the largest body of water in the world?

A.   The Pacific Ocean
B.   The Indian Ocean
C.   The Arctic Ocean
D.   The Atlantic Ocean

Answer: A, The biggest body of water in the world is the Pacific Ocean at 161.8 million km^2 (squared)

20. What is the smallest country when measured by total land area?

A.   Tuvalu
B.   Vatican City
C.   Maldives
D.   Monaco

Answer: B, Vatican City is the smallest country in the world

21. The United Kingdom is comprised of how many countries?

A.   6
B.   8
C.   4
D.   5

Answer: C, the United Kingdom is comprised of 4 different countries

22. The biggest desert in the world is:

A.   The Arabian
B.   The Great Australian
C.   The Sahara
D.   The Namib

Answer: C, the Sahara Desert is the largest desert in the world

23. How many great lakes are there located in Canada and the USA?

A.   2
B.   5
C.   3
D.   7

Answer: B, there are 5 lakes: Superior, Huron, Michigan, Erie and Ontario

24. Which is the world's highest mountain?

A.   Everest
B.   Kilimanjaro
C.   K2
D.   Makulu

Answer: A, Mt. Everest is the highest mountain in the world located in Nepal

25. Which river flows through the Grand Canyon?

A.   Nile River
B.   Colorado River
C.   Missouri River
D.   Yukon River

Answer: B, the Colorado River runs through the Grand Canyon

26. What is the capital city of Spain?

A.   Barcelona
B.   Madrid
C.   Granada
D.   Seville

Answer: B, Madrid is the capital of Spain with a population of 3.3 million people

27. What is the total height of Niagara Falls?

A.   125 feat
B.   57 feat
C.   312 feat
D.   167 feet

Answer: D, Niagara Falls stands at 167 feet tall at the highest point!

28. Who owns the land of Antarctica?

A.   USA
B.   Canada
C.   Russia
D.   None of the above

Answer: D, no one owns the land of Antarctica

29. Which Italian city is famous for its canals?

A.   Rome
B.   Venice
C.   Florence
D.   Milan

Answer: B, Venice is known for being built on water and having canals as its 'streets'

30. What are the only two countries to have a land border with the US?

A.   Canada and Mexico
B.   Canada and Cuba
C.   Canada and Spain
D.   Mexico and Brazil

Answer: A, Canada is located above the USA and Mexico is below on a map

HISTORY TRIVIA

"The more you know about the past, the better prepared you are for the future" - Theodore Roosevelt

1. World War I began in which year?

A.   1925
B.   1919
C.   1914
D.   1945

Answer: C, WWI began shortly after the assassination of Arch-Duke Ferdinand in 1914

2. Adolf Hitler was born in which country?

A.   Croatia
B.   Slovenia
C.   Germany

D.   Austria

Answer: D, Hitler was born in Lintz, Austria near the German border

3. In what city was John F. Kennedy assassinated in?

A.   Washington
B.   Dallas
C.   Austin
D.   Miami

Answer: B, JFK was assassinated while driving through Dallas in November 1963

4. When did the Cold War officially end?

A.   1889
B.   1990
C.   1989
D.   1979

Answer: C, the cold war officially ended in 1989

5. Published after her death, what did teenager Anne Frank leave behind?

A.   A dress
B.   A diary
C.   A bow
D.   A List

Answer: B, Anne Frank left behind a diary

6. Who was the first President of the United States?

A.   George Washington
B.   John Adams
C.   Barrack Obama
D.   Donald Trump

Answer: A, George Washington was the first person to be named president of the United States in 1789

7. What influential person became President of South Africa in 1994?

A.   Christopher Columbus
B.   Martin Luther King Jr.

C.   Nelson Mandela
D.   Michelangelo

Answer: C, Nelson Mandela became president of South Africa in 1994

8. Whose exploration of the New World had its quincentenary (500 year anniversary) in 1992?

A.   Marco Polo
B.   Christopher Columbus
C.   Ferdinand Magellan
D.   James Cook

Answer: B, Christopher Columbus

9. This famous Civil Rights Movement leader is famous for a speech that starts with "I have a dream..." - what is their name?

A.   Malcolm X
B.   Abraham Lincoln
C.   Martin Luther King Jr.
D.   Rosa Parks

Answer: C, "I have a dream," was the beginning of a

speech by Martin Luther King Jr. which he delivered in 1963 for people to hear

10. Which 4 presidents' faces can be found at Mt. Rushmore?

A.   George Washington, Jimmy Carter, Abraham Lincoln and Franklin D. Roosevelt
B.   Theodore Roosevelt, Franklin D. Roosevelt, Ronald Reagan, George Bush
C.   Richard Nixon, John F. Kennedy Jr., Bill Clinton, Thomas Jefferson
D.   Thomas Jefferson, George Washington, Theodore Roosevelt, and Abraham Lincoln

Answer: D, the presidents carved into Mount Rushmore are Thomas Jefferson, George Washington, Theodore Roosevelt, and Abraham Lincoln

11. When did the American Civil War take place?

A.   1961 - 1965
B.   1900 - 1904
C.   1861 - 1865
D.   1856 - 1860

Answer: C, the American Civil War took place 1861 - 1865

12. What was the Mayflower and what did it carry?

A.   A train with English Immigrants
B.   A ship carrying English Separatists
C.   A flower that symbolized something important
D.   A plane that flew around the world

Answer: B, the Mayflower was the ship that carried English Separatists to the New World now known as America

13. Who was the Prime Minister of Britain during World War II?

A.   Donald Trump
B.   Clement Attlee
C.   Franklin D. Roosevelt
D.   Winston Churchill

Answer: D, Attlee took over from Churchill after the war. He was only the second Prime Minister to be a member of the Labour Party

14. Who was the leader of the U.S.S.R. during World War II?

A. Emperor Hirohito
B. Joseph Stalin
C. Emperor Akihito
D. Vladimir Lenin

Answer: B, while Lenin was the first communist leader of Russia, Stalin served as their leader during World War II

15. Who were the ancient people responsible for building the pyramids?

A. American people
B. British people
C. Egyptian people
D. European people

Answer: C, the Egyptians built the great pyramids in Egypt

16. In which town was Jesus born?

A. Paris
B. Bethlehem
C. Amsterdam
D. Washington

Answer: B, Jesus was born in the town of Bethlehem

17. What are the Wright brothers famously known for?

A.   Flying the first powered aircraft
B.   Driving the first powered car
C.   Creating the first powered boat
D.   Building the first powered train

Answer: A, the Wright brothers flew the first powered aircraft on December 17th, 1903

18. Which country was the first one to use paper money?

A.   Egypt
B.   China
C.   Switzerland
D.   Denmark

Answer: B, China first used paper money during the Tang Dynasty in A.D. 618-907

19. Who invented the light bulb?

A.   Thomas Edison
B.   Isaac Newton
C.   Abraham Lincoln
D.   Winston Churchill

Answer: A, Thomas Edison invented the light bulb in 1879

20. Alexander Graham Bell invented which of the following devices?

A.   Telephone
B.   Airplane
C.   Car
D.   Train

Answer: A, he invented the telephone in 1876

21. Which city was divided by a wall from 1961 to 1989?

A.   Rome
B.   London
C.   Berlin
D.   Munich

Answer: C, the famous Berlin Wall was enforced on the people of Berlin from 1961 to 1989

22. Which US Apollo mission was the first to land on the moon?

A.   11
B.   13
C.   10
D.   9

Answer: A, Apollo 11 was the first spaceflight to land humans on the moon

23. Who was the first man on the moon?

A.   Buzz Aldrin
B.   Neil Armstrong
C.   Alan Shepard
D.   Tim Allen

Answer: B, Neil Armstrong was the first man on the moon on July 16th, 1969

24. Who drafted the Declaration of Independence?

A.   Abraham Lincoln
B.   George Washington
C.   Neil Armstrong
D.   Thomas Jefferson

Answer: D, Thomas Jefferson drafted the document and it was published in July of 1776

25. In which country were the modern Olympic Games held for the first time?

A.   Spain
B.   Greece
C.   Florence
D.   London

Answer: B, Greece was the first place to hold the modern Olympic Games

26. What famously happened to the Titanic in 1912?

A.   It sunk
B.   It caught on fire
C.   It blew up
D.   It was built

Answer: A, in 1912, the Titanic hit an iceberg and sank

27. What is the name of the building where the US president lives?

A.   Blue House
B.   Red House
C.   White House
D.   Big House

Answer: C, the White House is where the US president lives

28. Where can the famous building - the Empire State Building - be found?

A.   Atlanta
B.   Los Angeles
C.   Dallas
D.   New York

Answer: D, the Empire State Building is located in New York

29. What do the stars on the US flag represent?

A.   The cities in the USA
B.   The states in the USA
C.   The rivers in the USA
D.   The mountains in the USA

Answer: B, the stars on the American flag represent the different states in the USA

30. Who wrote the most performed plays of all time, such as Hamlet, Macbeth, Othello?

A.   Edgar Allen Poe
B.   Robert Frost
C.   William Shakespeare
D.   Ludwig Van Beethoven

Answer: C, William Shakespeare wrote Hamlet, Macbeth, Othello and many others

31. What is the famous prison called in California that is located on an Island, surrounded by water?

A.   Federal Correctional Complex
B.   United States Penitentiary
C.   Alcatraz

D.   Gulags

Answer: C, Alcatraz was built on an island off the coast of San Francisco

SCIENCE AND NATURE TRIVIA

"There is no better designer than nature." - Alexander Mcqueen

1. Our atmosphere is kept wrapped around the Earth by a:

A.   Moving weather pattern
B.   Magnetic field
C.   Constant pressure from space
D.   Gravitational pull

Answer: B, the atmosphere is kept close to the earth by a magnetic field

2. Most places on Earth experience:

A.   Droughts
B.   Excessive winds
C.   Rainy seasons
D.   Four seasons

Answer: D, most places on earth experience four seasons

3. What percentage of the Earth is covered in water?

A.   20%
B.   30%
C.   70%
D.   100%

Answer: C, 70% of our Earth is covered in water with land only accounting for the other 30%

4. In our solar system, earth is the _____ planet from our sun.

A.   2nd
B.   1st
C.   6th
D.   3rd

Answer: D, Earth is the 3rd planet from our sun

5. What can be found on earth that no other planet in our

solar system possesses?

A.   Water
B.   Seasons
C.   Sunlight
D.   Life

Answer: D, life makes our planet unique from the rest

6. Earth is the _____largest planet in our solar system.

A.   2nd
B.   9th
C.   5th
D.   10th

Answer: C, Earth is the 5th largest planet in our solar system

7. What are the two main metals in the Earth's core?

A.   Gold and silver
B.   Silver and iron
C.   Iron and platinum
D.   Iron and nickel

Answer: D, iron and nickel are the two main metals found in the Earth's core

8. What do you call a person who studies rocks?

A.   Geologist
B.   Meteorologist
C.   Rockologist
D.   Zoologist

Answer: A, a geologist studies rocks

9. What part of the plant conducts photosynthesis?

A.   Trunk
B.   Flower
C.   Leaf
D.   Branch

Answer: C, the leaf conducts photosynthesis

10. What is the boiling point of water?

A.   25 degrees Celsius
B.   100 degrees Celsius
C.   0 degrees Celsius
D.   70 degrees Celsius

Answer: B, 100 degrees Celsius is the boiling point of water

11. What body part helps pump blood throughout the body?

A.   Brain
B.   Heart
C.   Lungs
D.   Liver

Answer: B, the heart is the pump within your body when it comes to blood!

12. The three states of matter are solid, liquid and
_____

A.   Fire
B.   Water
C.   Gas

D.   Heat

Answer: C, gas is the last possible state for matter to be found in

13. What does boiling water turn into?

A.   Snow
B.   Clouds
C.   Mist
D.   Steam

Answer: D, boiling water turns into steam

14. What group of animals has scales on their bodies?

A.   Reptiles
B.   Amphibians
C.   Mammals
D.   Humans

Answer: A, reptiles have scales on them

15. What nutrient is the source of muscle building?

A.   Carbohydrates
B.   Fiber
C.   Protein
D.   Sugar

Answer: C, protein helps us build muscle

16. What gas do plants need in order to perform photosynthesis?

A.   Carbon dioxide
B.   Oxygen
C.   Ammonia
D.   Carbon monoxide

Answer: A, carbon dioxide is what plants need in order to perform photosynthesis

17. What are the layers of gases that surround the earth called?

A.   Ozone
B.   Hydrosphere
C.   Atmosphere
D.   Omnisphere

Answer: C, the atmosphere surrounds the earth

18. What do similar blood cells form when they group together?

A.   Tissue
B.   Organs
C.   Bone
D.   Teeth

Answer: A, when blood cells group together they form tissue

19. When animals eat both plants and meat, what are they called?

A.   Vegetarians
B.   Herbivores
C.   Omnivores
D.   Carnivores

Answer: C, omnivores feast on anything from plants to other animals

20. Biology is the study of what?

A.   Earth
B.   Living things
C.   Plants
D.   Dead things

Answer: B, biologists study plants, animals, and anything that is alive in the universe

21. What are considered the basic building blocks of all living things?

A.   Cells
B.   Atoms
C.   Electrons
D.   Organisms

Answer: A, all living things are made up of one or more cells.

22. Which of the following Is most responsible for the weather on earth?

A.   The ocean
B.   The sun
C.   The moon

D.   Global warming

Answer: B, even though the sun is far away, its heat gives Earth's atmosphere the energy to move, creating weather

23. Which of the following is NOT a layer of the Earth?

A.   Mantle
B.   Crust
C.   Inner Core
D.   Plate

Answer: D, the Earth's layers include the core, mantle, outer core, and inner core

24. What galaxy do we live in?

A.   Black eye galaxy
B.   Cartwheel galaxy
C.   Milky Way Galaxy
D.   Oreo Galaxy

Answer: C, our solar system is a part of the Milky Way Galaxy

25. What are igneous rocks made out of?

A.   Smaller rocks
B.   Salt
C.   Crystals
D.   Sand

Answer: C, igneous rocks form when magma cools and crystalizes

26. Which of the following is NOT part of the scientific method?

A.   Experimentation
B.   Manipulation
C.   Data Collection
D.   Hypothesis

Answer: B, the scientific method steps are: Question, Research, Hypothesis, Experiment, Collect Data, Analysis, Conclusion

27. What is yeast?

A.   A plant
B.   An animal
C.   A bacterium
D.   A fungus

Answer: D, yeast is a type of fungus

28. A single piece of DNA is called what?

A.   Chromosome
B.   Nucleus
C.   Ribosome
D.   Cytoplasm

Answer: A, a single piece of DNA is called a chromosome

29. What was once considered a planet in our solar system but is now considered a dwarf planet?

A.   Venus
B.   Pluto
C.   Centauri b
D.   Jupiter

Answer: B, Pluto was once considered a full-sized planet but it now considered a dwarf planet

30. What system of the body controls the senses?

A. Circulatory system
B. Nervous system
C. Skeletal system
D. Digestive system

Answer: B, the nervous system controls the senses within the body

31. How many colors are rainbows comprised of?

A. 4
B. 3
C. 2
D. 7

Answer: D, rainbows have 7 colors: red, orange, yellow, green, blue, indigo, violet

SPORTS TRIVIA

"Sports do not build character; they reveal it" - John Woode

1. In what sport is the word 'love' used?

A.   Ice hockey
B.   Basketball
C.   Tennis
D.   Baseball

Answer: C, tennis uses the word love to describe zero points

2. What type of race is the Tour de France?

A.   Running
B.   Biking
C.   Walking
D.   Swimming

Answer: B, the Tour de France is a biking race

3. What is Canada's national winter sport?

A.   Ice hockey
B.   Volleyball
C.   Lacrosse
D.   Soccer

Answer: A, ice hockey is Canada's national winter sport

4. What is the name of the championship series that the National Basketball Association has to end the playoffs?

A.   NBA Finals
B.   World basketball series
C.   World basketball championship
D.   NBA Playoffs

Answer: A, the championship in the NBA is called the NBA Finals

5. Which golf club is used when players want to hit the ball as far as possible?

A.   Sand Wedge
B.   Iron
C.   Putter
D.   Driver

Answer: D, a driver is used to hit a golf ball as far as possible

6. What is the area called where baseball players watch their team play from?

A.   Den
B.   Bullpen
C.   Stands
D.   Dugout

Answer: D, baseball players watch their fellow teammates play from the dugout

7. What is soccer's international championship games called?

A.   Global Football Championship
B.   Soccer Playoffs
C.   World Cup
D.   World Series

Answer: C, the international soccer championship games is called the World Cup

8. How many periods are in an ice hockey game?

A.   2
B.   3
C.   1
D.   4

Answer: B, ice hockey is made up of 3 periods. However, at the NHL level, if both teams are tied at the end of the 3rd period, the game will go into a 4th period called 'overtime'

9. In football, what is the name of the trophy that the Super Bowl winners receive?

A.   Stanley Cup
B.   Vince Lombardi Trophy
C.   Grey Cup
D.   NFL Cup

Answer: B, the name of the trophy is called the Vince Lombardi Trophy which was first awarded in 1967

10. What sport was Michael Jordan famous for?

A.   Basketball
B.   Football
C.   Baseball
D.   Cricket

Answer: A, Michael Jordan was famous for basketball. However, he did try his hand at baseball as well but never really made a name for himself in that sport

11. What sport did Michael Phelps compete in during the Olympic games?

A.   Ice hockey
B.   Swimming
C.   Table tennis
D.   Track & Field

Answer: B, Michael Phelps competed in swimming events throughout his Olympic career

12. Where would you see a pommel horse?

A.   Horseback riding
B.   Cricket
C.   Gymnastics
D.   Tennis

Answer: C, gymnastics uses a pommel horse.

13. A caddie carries around a bag for what type of athlete?

A.   A golfer
B.   A cricket player
C.   A field hockey player
D.   A water polo player

Answer: A, golfers have assistants called caddies who carry their golf club bags for them and help them with decisions on shots

14. How many pins do you have to knock down to get a

strike in bowling?

A.   8
B.   10
C.   12
D.   6

Answer: B, you have to knock down 10 pins in bowling to get a strike

15. Of these 4 answers, which one is NOT a golf term?

A.   Home Run
B.   Birdie
C.   Bogey
D.   Par

Answer: A, a home run is a term used in baseball and cricket when a player hits a ball out of the playing area

16. If you throw a strike, make a spare or throw a gutter ball, you are playing what sport?

A.   Bowling
B.   Basketball

C.   Golf
D.   Track & Field

Answer: A, the terms gutter ball, spare and strike are all from the sport of bowling

17. What do you put on the end of your cue stick in order to ensure you make clean contact with the cue ball?

A.   Water
B.   Tar
C.   Oil
D.   Chalk

Answer: D, chalk is used on the ends of cue sticks in order to make sure the cue ball and the cue have clean contact

18. Which of these sports does not use a net?

A.   Soccer
B.   Golf
C.   Tennis
D.   Volleyball

Answer: B, golf does not use nets unlike the other three sports

19. What is the name of the playing area in which boxing matches are held?

A.   Diamond
B.   Field
C.   Court
D.   Ring

Answer: D, boxers fight in an area called 'the ring'

20. Crawl, backstroke and butterfly are different methods in which sport?

A.   Track & field
B.   Swimming
C.   Water polo
D.   Skiing

Answer: B, swimming uses these terms as they are methods of swimming lengths in the pool

21. Which sport uses the term slam dunk?

A.   Baseball
B.   Wrestling
C.   Basketball
D.   Darts

Answer: C, basketball uses the term slam dunk for when a player jumps and slams the ball through the hoop of the basketball net

22. Dump, floater and wipe are terms used in which team sport?

A.   Basketball
B.   Biking
C.   Rock Skipping
D.   Volleyball

Answer: D, volleyball utilizes the terms dump, floater and wipe

23. A tennis game with one player on each side of the net is called?

A.   A singles match
B.   A doubles match
C.   A two person
D.   Head on match

Answer: A, a tennis match with one player on each side of the net is called a singles match

24. In NASCAR, what does the term "groove" mean?

A.   Getting fresh tires
B.   Practice of racing nose to tail
C.   Strategy of pitting week before running out
D.   Best route around the track

Answer: D, "groove" is a slang term for the best route around the racetrack. The "high groove" takes a car close to the outside wall, while the "low groove" stays closer to the apron

25. In golf, what do you call a score of 4 under par on any given hole?

A.   A pelican
B.   An eagle
C.   A condor
D.   A turkey

Answer: C, a "condor" is the name for a score of 4 under par

26. Whose ear did Mike Tyson bite off during a 1997 boxing match?

A.   Buster Douglas
B.   Evander Holyfield
C.   Lennox lewis
D.   Floyd Mayweather

Answer: B, during his fight against Evander Holyfield in 1997, Mike Tyson was disqualified after biting off part of Holyfield's ear

27. What sport uses a broom?

A.   Slamball
B.   Cricket
C.   Wakeboarding
D.   Curling

Answer: D, curling uses a broom to sweep the ice surface in the path of the stone to speed it up or slow it down

28. Squash is a member of which sport family?

A. Football
B. Running sports
C. Water sports
D. Racket sports

Answer: D, squash is a racket sport played in a four-walled court with a small, hollow rubber ball

29. What sports league awards the Art Ross trophy to the player who leads the league in points?

A. National Hockey League
B. Major League of Soccer
C. National Basketball Association
D. National Football League

Answer: A, the Art Ross Trophy is awarded to the National Hockey League (NHL) player who leads the league in points at the end of the regular season

30. What player was nicknamed "Mr. Hockey"?

A. Mark Messier
B. Gordie Howe
C. Bobby Orr
D. Wayne Gretsky

Answer: B, nicknamed "Mr. Hockey", Gordie Howe is considered the most complete player to ever play the game and one of the greatest ice hockey players of all time

MATH TRIVIA

1. What description best suits the characteristics of a rectangle?

A.   Equal on all sides
B.   Round on all sides and no 90 degree angles
C.   2 sides of equal length and two shorter sides of equal length
D.   3 sides in total

Answer: C, a rectangle has 2 sides of equal length and two shorter sides of equal length.

2. What is the next prime number after 7?

A.   8

B.   11
C.   9
D.   12

Answer: B, 11 is the next prime number after 7

3. How many eggs would you have if you bought half a dozen?

A.   4
B.   5
C.   6
D.   12

Answer: C, a traditional dozen is equal to 12, so, half a dozen would be 6 since 6 is half of 12

4. How many textbooks are on a bus of 20 children with 5 textbooks each?

A.   60 textbooks
B.   100 textbooks
C.   150 textbooks
D.   20 textbooks

Answer: B, 100 textbooks would be on the bus since 20

times 5 equals 100!

5. If an item costs $2.00 and there's a "buy three get one extra free" sale on it, how much do four cost?

A. $10.00
B. $8.00
C. $12.00
D. $6.00

Answer: D, since the 4th one is free, you would times 2 by 3 and you get $6.00

6. If 1GB of memory can hold 350 songs, how many songs can 2GB of memory hold?

A.   500
B.   700
C.   1000
D.   600

Answer: B, since 350 times 2 equals 700

7. What would you get back for change on a $4.52 purchase if you paid with a $5 bill?

A.   50 cents
B.   1 dollar
C.   48 cents
D.   1 dollar 48 cents

Answer: C, since $5.00 minus $4.52 equals $0.48

8. If Joan buys a candy bar for $0.50 every day, how much will she spend on candy in 2 weeks?

A. $6
B. $14
C. $12
D. $7

Answer: D, since 14 days (which is 2 weeks) times 0.50 equals 7!

9. How many cookies should be given to each of 9 children to evenly share a box of 27?

A.   3
B.   5
C.   4
D.   10

Answer: A, 3 cookies would be given to each child since 27 divided by 9 equals 3

10. If the teacher has 28 students in her class, how many are absent if only 23 chairs are filled?

A.   28
B.   23
C.   5
D.   7

Answer: C, there would be 5 students missing since 28 total students minus 23 full chairs equals 5 students missing

11. In math, what does the word "sum" mean?

A.   Multiplication
B.   Division
C.   Addition
D.   Subtraction

Answer: C, sums are addition problems

12. In math, what does the word "minus" mean?

A.   Addition
B.   Subtraction
C.   Multiplication
D.   Division

Answer: B, minus refers to the act of subtracting a number from another number

13. If Max has $50 and each shirt costs $10, how many shirts can Max buy?

A.   10
B.   5
C.   7
D.   15

Answer: B, since 50 divided by 10 equals 5, that means Max can buy 5 shirts!

14. What is the top number of a fraction called?

A.   Numerator
B.   Denominator

C.   Top Number
D.   Instigator

Answer: A, the top number of a fraction is called the numerator

15. What is a shape with 8 sides called?

A.   Hexagon
B.   Polygon
C.   Octagon
D.   Square

Answer: C, an octagon, since 'oct' means 8

16. What is the next prime number after 3?

A.   7
B.   11
C.   15
D.   5

Answer: D, 5 is the next prime number after 3

17. What does the term 'century' represent?

A.   10 years
B.   100 years
C.   1000 years
D.   5000 years

Answer: B, a century represents 100 consecutive years

18. What are integers?

A.   Odd Numbers
B.   Even numbers
C.   Do not include fractions
D.   Are fractions

Answers: C, integers are similar to whole numbers and also include negative numbers, but do not include fractions

19. What is the sum of the angles of a triangle?

A.   90 degrees
B.   200 degrees
C.   180 degrees

D.   300 degrees

Answer: C, 180 degrees is the sum of all angles of a triangle

20. What do you call a triangle with different sides?

A.   Scalene triangle
B.   Isosceles triangle
C.   Acute
D.   Equilateral

Answer: A, a triangle with different sides is called a scalene triangle

21. Which polygon has the least number of sides?

A.   Square
B.   Quadrilateral
C.   Triangle
D.   Octagon

Answer: C, a triangle has the least amount of sides of all polygons with only 3 sides

22. How many points are there on a pentagon?

A. 3
B. 2
C. 8
D. 5

Answer: D, there are 5 points and sides on a pentagon. 'Penta' means 5

23. The perimeter of a circle is also known as what?

A. Circumference
B. Polynomial
C. Radius
D. Length

Answer: A, the perimeter of a circle is also known as the circumference

25. John has 21 apples and needs to divide them amongst 7 people evenly. How many apples will each person get?

A. 5
B. 3

C.   2
D.   1

Answer: B, 3 apples would go to each person because 21 divided by 7 equals 3

26. Lucas has $27. He spent $7 at the corner store and another $10 on a t-shirt. How much money does Lucas have left over?

A. $5
B. $7
C. $11
D. $10

Answer: D, Lucas has $10 left over since $27 minus $7 equals $20 and then another $10 minus $20 equals $10

27. If Alex drove north 50 kilometers, then drove south 10 kilometers and then drove north another 20 kilometers, how far did he end up going?

A.   60 kilometers
B.   40 kilometers
C.   80 kilometers
D.   100 kilometers

Answer: A, 60 kilometers would be the total distance Alex drove

28. The term 'product' refers to what form of math?

A.   Substraction
B.   Addition
C.   Multiplication
D.   Division

Answer: C, the answer to a multiplication problem is called the product

29. How many faces does a cube have?

A.   2
B.   4
C.   6
D.   8

Answer: C, a cube has 6 different faces in total

30. What are the corners of a shape also known as?

A.   Faces
B.   Angles
C.   Edges
D.   Vertices

Answer: D, the corners of a shape can also be called 'Vertices'

CONCLUSION

Wow! You made it through all of the trivia and multiple choice questions in *Trivia for Smart Kids*. How did you end up doing? These trivia questions are some of our personal favorites and have had huge impacts on people all around the world. We hope they had the same effect on you!

Once again, we would like to thank you for reading our book *Trivia for Smart Kids* and can't wait to hear what you thought about it. If you enjoyed listening to this book, please don't forget to leave a review and let us know how much you loved it. Reviews mean the world to us and help us continue to create books just like this one for years to come.

Keep an eye out for Trivia For Smart Kids Part 2!

Thank you!

DL Digital Entertainment

Made in the USA
Las Vegas, NV
06 January 2022